SUNRISE

More poetry anthologies available
from Macmillan Collector's Library

Poems for New Parents edited by Becky Brown

Happy Hour introduced by Jancis Robinson

Poems for Stillness introduced by Ana Sampson

Poems of the Sea introduced by Adam Nicolson

Poems for Happiness introduced by Richard Coles

Poems for Travellers introduced by Paul Theroux

Poems for Christmas introduced by Judith Flanders

Poems of Childhood introduced by Michael Morpurgo

Poems on Nature introduced by Helen Macdonald

Poems for Love introduced by Joanna Trollope

SUNRISE

Poems to Kick-Start Your Day

Edited and introduced by
SUSIE GIBBS

MACMILLAN COLLECTOR'S LIBRARY

This collection first published 2022 by Macmillan Collector's Library
an imprint of Pan Macmillan
The Smithson, 6 Briset Street, London ECIM 5NR
EU representative: Macmillan Publishers Ireland Ltd, 1st Floor,
The Liffey Trust Centre, 117–126 Sheriff Street Upper,
Dublin 1, DO1 YC43
Associated companies throughout the world
www.panmacmillan.com

ISBN 978-1-5290-9133-5

The permissions acknowledgements on p. 167 constitute an
extension of this copyright page.

1 3 5 7 9 8 6 4 2

A CIP catalogue record for this book is available from the British Library.

Cover and endpaper design: Katie Tooke, Pan Macmillan Art Department
Typeset in Plantin by Jouve (UK), Milton Keynes
Printed and bound in China by Imago

Visit **www.panmacmillan.com** to read more
about all our books and to buy them.

Contents

PURPOSE

PERSEVERANCE

EMPATHY

vii

WISDOM

PERSPECTIVE

CONTENTMENT

Preface

SUSIE GIBBS

'Awake! Glad heart! Get up and sing!'
Henry Vaughan (1621–95)

The simple joy and renewed hope of the sun rising every day is a gift that we can all too easily overlook. For many of us, the siren call of emails, texts and social media shapes our morning routine; for others, the mad morning timetable affords no time for anything other than getting somewhere on time. *Sunrise* offers a range from the really very short indeed to longer, more reflective poems, so whoever and wherever you are, these poems are for you – to inspire you to greet each new day with optimism and confidence. Think of them as pain-free exercises, daily workouts to help you cope, something to sustain you through the tough times. They will help build your spiritual and emotional resilience, replenishing your reserves for when you need them. Think big, but value the detail. Don't beat yourself up. Take charge. Be good. Lose yourself in simple beauties. Use the rhythm of the words to meditate. A poem that speaks to you is a gift – look after it, treasure it, hold it in your pocket like a smoothly rounded pebble, worn by millennia of wind and waves, and feel the comfort it offers when you close your fingers around it – a talisman against a rainy day. And remember, in our gloriously circular world, it's always, always sunrise somewhere.

These poems contain tried and tested truths, positive and thought-provoking, regardless of historical context.

They draw on the time-proven wisdom of our poetic heritage, countless experiences, insights and conclusions. It is sometimes said that poetry is often born of trauma and loss. The action of putting painful things into words can, of course, be cathartic, and it is comforting to read about how other people cope with similar experiences and issues. But whilst sorrow must inevitably take up some room in the potentially limitless library of our mind, it is important that it is balanced by shelves full of positive, grateful, appreciative and inspiring material. Life is full of anxieties, from the minute to the global, and we need to rebuff these with a stable and robust state of mental health, which is itself something that needs to be cultivated and nurtured. I hope that regular reading of the poems in this book will help you form healthy habits of mind, to become a virtuoso of positive thinking, looking outward, not inward, for inspiration.

I cannot remember a time when there was not a copy of the 'Desiderata' (see p. 140) on the kitchen wall of wherever I was living; as a result, I know most of it by heart. At some point in my life I realized that it was useful to have a few poems up my sleeve. Whether sitting in the dentist's chair, slogging it out on a running machine, trying to clear my mind when unable to sleep, or even as a desperate party turn, poetry has always been a tool for me, something I have used as a support.

Not all of these poems will speak to all readers. 'Inspiration' is not one size fits all, but if even a single poem speaks to you, inspires you, stays with you, and maybe even becomes something to be learnt and turned to when times are tough, then, yes, *Sunrise* has succeeded. Some poems are more taxing, requiring a little more thought and concentration to winkle out their meaning, but most are undemanding enough to assimilate with the speed we expect in today's crazy and exciting world. Dip in, roam about, find something that suits you – and read. And think about it. Savour it. Read it again. And maybe even once more. Find the inspiration, and take it with you into the day that awaits you.

Every new day is untouched, full of promise and possibility. Make the most of it. Nurture your stability. Reboot your soul. Harness the equilibrium of the day and read yourself ready for the day ahead.

> *'There was never a night or a problem*
> *that could defeat sunrise or hope.'*
>
> Bernard Williams (1929–2003)

To-day

So here hath been dawning
Another blue day:
Think, wilt thou let it
Slip useless away?

Thomas Carlyle (1795–1881)

HOPE

'Piled for burning'

Piled for burning,
brushwood
starts to bud.

Bonchō (1640–1714)

from Rubáiyát of Omar Khayyám

I

Awake! for Morning in the Bowl of Night
Has flung the Stone that puts the Stars to Flight:
    And Lo! the Hunter of the East has caught
The Sultán's Turret in a Noose of Light.

II

Dreaming when Dawn's Left Hand was in the Sky
I heard a Voice within the Tavern cry,
    'Awake, my Little ones, and fill the Cup
'Before Life's Liquor in its Cup be dry.'

III

And, as the Cock crew, those who stood before
The Tavern shouted—'Open then the Door!
    'You know how little while we have to stay,
        'And, once departed, may return no more.'
        [...]

XXXVII

Ah, fill the Cup:—what boots it to repeat
How Time is slipping underneath our feet:
    Unborn To-morrow, and dead Yesterday,
Why fret about them if To-day be sweet!

Edward Fitzgerald (1809–1883)

New Day

The day is so new
You can hear it yawning,
Listen:

The new day
is yawning
and stretching

and waiting to start.

In the clear blue sky
I hear the new day's heart.

Ian McMillan (1956–)

from Song of Solomon

For, lo, the winter is past
The rain is over and gone;
The flowers appear on the earth;
The time of the singing of birds is come
And the voice of the turtle dove is
    heard in our land.

Written in March

The cock is crowing,
The stream is flowing,
The small birds twitter,
The lake doth glitter,
The green field sleeps in the sun;
    The oldest and youngest
    Are at work with the strongest;
    The cattle are grazing,
    Their heads never raising;
There are forty feeding like one!

    Like an army defeated
    The snow hath retreated,
    And now doth fare ill
    On the top of the bare hill;
The ploughboy is whooping – anon – anon:
    There's joy in the mountains;
    There's life in the fountains;
    Small clouds are sailing,
    Blue sky prevailing;
The rain is over and gone!

William Wordsworth (1770–1850)

from The Earthly Paradise

Slayer of the winter, art thou here again?
O welcome, thou that bring'st the summer nigh!
The bitter wind makes not thy victory vain,
Nor will we mock thee for thy faint blue sky.
Welcome, O March! whose kindly days and dry
Make April ready for the throstle's song.
Thou first redresser of the winter's wrong!

Yea, welcome March! and though I die ere June,
Yet for the hope of life I give thee praise,
Striving to swell the burden of the tune
That even now I hear thy brown birds raise,
Unmindful of the past or coming days;
Who sing: 'O joy! a new year is begun:
What happiness to look upon the sun!'

Ah, what begetteth all this storm of bliss
But Death himself, who crying solemnly,
E'en from the heart of sweet Forgetfulness,
Bids us 'Rejoice, lest pleasureless ye die.
Within a little time must ye go by.
Stretch forth your open hands, and while ye live
Take all the gifts that Death and Life may give.'

William Morris (1834–1896)

from Revolution

West and away the wheels of darkness roll,
 Day's beamy banner up the east is borne,
Spectres and fears, the nightmare and her foal,
 Drown in the golden deluge of the morn.

A. E. Housman (1859–1936)

Music

Let me go where'er I will
I hear a sky-born music still:
It sounds from all things old,
It sounds from all things young;
From all that's fair, from all that's foul,
Peals out a cheerful song.
It is not only in the rose,
It is not only in the bird,
Not only where the rainbow glows,
Nor in the song of woman heard,
But in the darkest, meanest things
There always, always something sings.
'Tis not in the high stars alone,
Nor in the cups of budding flowers,
Nor in the redbreast's mellow tone,
Nor in the bow that smiles in showers,
But in the mud and scum of things
There always, always something sings.

Ralph Waldo Emerson (1803–1882)

The Strange Music

Other loves may sink and settle, other loves may loose
    and slack,
But I wander like a minstrel with a harp upon his
    back,
Though the harp be on my bosom, though I finger
    and I fret,
Still, my hope is all before me: for I cannot play
    it yet.

In your strings is hid a music that no hand hath e'er
    let fall,
In your soul is sealed a pleasure that you have not
    known at all;
Pleasure subtle as your spirit, strange and slender as
    your frame,
Fiercer than the pain that folds you, softer than your
    sorrow's name.

Not as mine, my soul's anointed, not as mine the
    rude and light
Easy mirth of many faces, swaggering pride of song
    and fight;
Something stranger, something sweeter, something
    waiting you afar,
Secret as your stricken senses, magic as your
    sorrows are.

But on this, God's harp supernal, stretched but to be
      stricken once,
Hoary time is a beginner, Life a bungler, Death a
      dunce.
But I will not fear to match them – no, by God, I will
      not fear,
I will learn you, I will play you and the stars stand
      still to hear.

G. K. Chesterton (1874–1936)

November

The leaves are fading and falling,
    The winds are rough and wild,
The birds have ceased their calling,
    But let me tell you, my child,

Though day by day, as it closes,
    Doth darker and colder grow,
The roots of the bright red roses
    Will keep alive in the snow.

And when the Winter is over,
    The boughs will get new leaves,
The quail come back to the clover,
    And the swallow back to the eaves.

The robin will wear on his bosom
    A vest that is bright and new,
And the loveliest way-side blossom
    Will shine with the sun and dew.

The leaves today are whirling,
    The brooks are dry and dumb,
But let me tell you, my darling,
    The Spring will be sure to come.

There must be rough, cold weather,
    And winds and rains so wild;
Not all good things together
    Come to us here, my child.

So, when some dear joy loses
    Its beauteous summer glow,
Think how the roots of the roses
    Are kept alive in the snow.

Alice Cary (1820–1871)

To-day

So here hath been dawning
Another blue day:
Think, wilt thou let it
Slip useless away?

Out of Eternity
This new day is born:
In to Eternity
At night will return.

Behold it aforetime
No eye ever did:
So soon it for ever
From all eyes is hid.

Here hath been dawning
Another blue day:
Think, wilt thou let it
Slip useless away?

Thomas Carlyle (1795–1881)

COURAGE

Courage

Dare to be true;
    Nothing can need a lie;
The fault that needs one most
    Grows two thereby.

George Herbert (1593–1633)

The Little Black-Eyed Rebel

A boy drove into the city, his wagon loaded down
With food to feed the people of the British-governed
    town;
And the little black-eyed rebel, so innocent and sly,
Was watching for his coming from the corner of
    her eye.

His face looked broad and honest, his hands were
    brown and tough,
The clothes he wore upon him were homespun,
    coarse, and rough;
But one there was who watched him, who long time
    lingered nigh
And cast at him sweet glances from the corner of
    her eye.

He drove up to the market, he waited in the line;
His apples and potatoes were fresh and fair and fine;
But long and long he waited, and no one came to
    buy,
Save the black-eyed rebel, watching from the corner
    of her eye.

"Now who will buy my apples?" he shouted, long and
    loud;
And "Who wants my potatoes?" he repeated to the
    crowd;
But from all the people round him came no word of
    a reply,
Save the black-eyed rebel, answering from the corner
    of her eye.

For she knew that 'neath the lining of the coat he
    wore that day,
Were long letters from the husbands and the fathers
    far away,
Who were fighting for the freedom that they meant to
    gain or die;
And a tear like silver glistened in the corner of
    her eye.

But the treasures–how to get them? crept the question
    through her mind,
Since keen enemies were watching for what prizes
    they might find;
And she paused a while and pondered, with a pretty
    little sigh;
Then resolve crept through her features, and a
    shrewdness fired her eye.

So she resolutely walked up to the wagon old and red;
"May I have a dozen apples for a kiss?" she sweetly
    said:
And the brown face flushed to scarlet; for the boy was
    somewhat shy,
And he saw her laughing at him from the corner of
    her eye.

"You may have them all for nothing, and more, if you
    want," quoth he.
"I will have them, my good fellow, but can pay for
    them," said she,
And she clambered on the wagon, minding not who
    all were by.
With a laugh of reckless romping in the corner of
    her eye.

Clinging round his brawny neck, she clasped her
    fingers white and small,
And then whispered, "Quick! the letters! thrust them
    underneath my shawl!
Carry back again *this* package, and be sure that you
    are spry!"
And she sweetly smiled upon him from the corner of
    her eye.

Loud the motley crowd were laughing at the strange,
    ungirlish freak.
And the boy was scared and panting, and so dashed
    he could not speak;
And, "Miss, *I* have good apples," a bolder lad did cry;
But she answered, "No, *I* thank you," from the corner
    of her eye.

With the news of loved ones absent to the dear
    friends they would greet,
Searching them who hungered for them, swift she
    glided through the street.
"There is nothing worth the doing that it does not
    pay to try,"
Thought the little black-eyed rebel, with a twinkle in
    her eye.

Will Carleton (1845–1912)

To Fortune

Tumble me down, and I will sit
Upon my ruins, smiling yet;
Tear me to tatters, yet I'll be
Patient in my necessity.
Laugh at my scraps of clothes, and shun
Me, as a feared infection;
Yet scarecrow-like I'll walk, as one
Neglecting thy derision.

Robert Herrick (1591–1674)

Invictus

Out of the night that covers me,
    Black as the pit from pole to pole,
I thank whatever gods may be
    For my unconquerable soul.

In the fell clutch of circumstance
    I have not winced nor cried aloud:
Under the bludgeonings of chance
    My head is bloody, but unbowed.

Beyond this place of wrath and tears
    Looms but the Horror of the shade,
And yet the menace of the years
    Finds and shall find me unafraid.

It matters not how strait the gate,
    How charged with punishments the scroll,
I am the master of my fate:
    I am the captain of my soul.

W. E. Henley (1849–1903)

Travel

The railroad track is miles away,
    And the day is loud with voices speaking,
Yet there isn't a train goes by all day
    But I hear its whistle shrieking.

All night there isn't a train goes by,
    Though the night is still for sleep and dreaming,
But I see its cinders red on the sky,
    And hear its engines steaming.

My heart is warm with the friends I make,
    And better friends I'll not be knowing,
Yet there isn't a train I wouldn't take,
    No matter where it's going.

Edna St. Vincent Millay (1892–1950)

No Enemies

You have no enemies, you say?
Alas, my friend, the boast is poor.
He who has mingled in the fray
Of duty, that the brave endure,
Must have made foes. If you have none,
Small is the work that you have done.
You've hit no traitor on the hip,
You've dashed no cup from perjured lip,
You've never turned the wrong to right,
You've been a coward in the fight.

Charles Mackay (1814–1889)

Lochinvar

O, young Lochinvar is come out of the west,
Through all the wide Border his steed was the best;
And save his good broadsword he weapons had none,
He rode all unarm'd, and he rode all alone.
So faithful in love, and so dauntless in war,
That never was knight like the young Lochinvar.

He staid not for brake, and he stopp'd not for stone,
He swam the Eske river where ford there was none;
But ere he alighted at Netherby gate,
The bride had consented, the gallant came late:
For a laggard in love, and a dastard in war,
Was to wed the fair Ellen of brave Lochinvar.

So boldly he enter'd the Netherby Hall,
Among bride's-men, and kinsmen, and brothers,
          and all:
Then spoke the bride's father, his hand on his sword
(For the poor craven bridegroom said never a word),
"O come ye in peace here, or come ye in war,
Or to dance at our bridal, young Lord Lochinvar?"

"I long woo'd your daughter, my suit you denied;—
Love swells like the Solway, but ebbs like its tide—
And now am I come, with this lost love of mine,
To lead but one measure, drink one cup of wine,
There are maidens in Scotland more lovely by far,
That would gladly be bride to the young Lochinvar."

The bride kiss'd the goblet: the knight took it up,
He quaff'd off the wine, and he threw down the cup,

She look'd down to blush, and she look'd up to sigh,
With a smile on her lips, and a tear in her eye.
He took her soft hand, ere her mother could bar,—
"Now tread we a measure!" said young Lochinvar.

So stately his form, and so lovely her face,
That never a hall such a galliard did grace;
While her mother did fret, and her father did fume,
And the bridegroom stood dangling his bonnet and
    plume;
And the bride-maidens whisper'd, "'Twere better
    by far,
To have match'd our fair cousin with young
    Lochinvar."

One touch of her hand, and one word in her ear,
When they reach'd the hall-door, and the charger
    stood near;
So light to the croupe the fair lady he swung,
So light to the saddle before her he sprung!
"She is won! we are gone, over bank, bush, and scaur;
They'll have fleet steeds that follow," quoth young
    Lochinvar.

There was mounting 'mong Graemes of the Netherby
    clan;
Forsters, Fenwicks, and Musgraves, they rode and
    they ran:
There was racing and chasing on Cannobie Lee,
But the lost bride of Netherby ne'er did they see.
So daring in love, and so dauntless in war,
Have ye e'er heard of gallant like young Lochinvar?

Sir Walter Scott (1771–1832)

Precious Stones

An emerald is as green as grass;
    A ruby red as blood;
A sapphire shines as blue as heaven;
    A flint lies in the mud.

A diamond is a brilliant stone,
    To catch the world's desire;
An opal holds a fiery spark;
    But a flint holds fire.

Christina Rossetti (1830–1894)

The Door

Go and open the door.
    Maybe outside there's
    a tree, or a wood,
    a garden,
    or a magic city.

Go and open the door.
    Maybe a dog's rummaging.
    Maybe you'll see a face,
or an eye,
or the picture
        of a picture.

Go and open the door.
    If there's a fog
    it will clear.

Go and open the door.
    Even if there's only
    the darkness ticking,
    even if there's only
    the hollow wind,
    even if
        nothing
            is there,
go and open the door.

At least
there'll be
a draught.

Miroslav Holub (1923–1998),
translated by Ian Milner and George Theiner

PURPOSE

'When the sun rises, I go to work'

When the sun rises, I go to work,
When the sun goes down, I take my rest,
I dig the well from which I drink,
I farm the soil that yields my food,
I share creation, Kings can do no more.

Anon. (Ancient China, 2500 BCE)

The King's Job

Once on a time was a King anxious to understand
What was the wisest thing a man could do for his
    land.
Most of his population hurried to answer the
    question,
Each with a long oration, each with a new suggestion.
They interrupted his meals—he wasn't safe in his bed
    from 'em—
They hung round his neck and heels, and at last His
    Majesty fled from 'em.
He put on a leper's cloak (people leave lepers alone),
Out of the window he broke, and abdicated his
    throne.
All that rapturous day, while his Court and his
    Ministers mourned him,
He danced on his own highway till his own Policemen
    warned him.
Gay and cheerful he ran (lepers don't cheer as a rule)
Till he found a philosopher-man teaching an
    infant-school.
The windows were open wide, the King sat down on
    the grass,
And heard the children inside reciting "Our King is
    an ass."
The King popped in his head: "Some people would
    call this treason,
But I think you are right," he said; "Will you kindly
    give me your reason?"
Lepers in school are as rare as kings with a leper's
    dress on,

But the class didn't stop or stare; it calmly went on
    with the lesson:
"The wisest thing, we suppose, that a man can do for his
    land,
Is the work that lies under his nose, with the tools that lie
    under his hand."
The King whipped off his cloak, and stood in his
    crown before 'em.
He said: "My dear little folk, *Ex ore parvulorum*—
(Which is Latin for "Children know more than
    grown-ups would credit")
You have shown me the road to go, and I propose to
    tread it."
Back to his Kingdom he ran, and issued a
    Proclamation,
"Let every living man return to his occupation!"
Then he explained to the mob who cheered in his
    palace and round it,
"I've been to look for a job, and Heaven be praised
    I've found it!"

                    Rudyard Kipling (1865–1936)

The Sluggard

'Tis the voice of the sluggard; I hear him complain,
'You have waked me too soon: I must slumber again.'
    As the door on its hinges, so he on his bed,
    Turns his sides, and his shoulders, and his heavy
       head.

'A little more sleep, and a little more slumber'–
Thus he wastes half his days, and his hours without
    number;
    And when he gets up, he sits folding his hands,
    Or walks about saunt'ring, or trifling he stands.

I passed by his garden, and saw the wild brier,
The thorn and the thistle grow broader and higher.
    The clothes that hang on him are turning to rags;
    And his money still wastes till he starves or he
      begs.

I made him a visit, still hoping to find
He had took better care for improving his mind.
    He told me his dreams, talked of eating and
      drinking.
    But he scarce reads his Bible, and never loves
      thinking.

Said I then to my heart: 'Here's a lesson for me;
That man's but a picture of what I might be;
    But thanks to my friends for their care in my
        breeding,
    Who taught me betimes to love working and
        reading.'

Isaac Watts (1674–1748)

Reveille

Wake: the silver dusk returning
    Up the beach of darkness brims,
And the ship of sunrise burning
    Strands upon the eastern rims.

    Wake: the vaulted shadow shatters,
      Trampled to the floor it spanned,
And the tent of night in tatters
    Straws the sky-pavilioned land.

Up, lad, up, 'tis late for lying:
    Hear the drums of morning play;
Hark, the empty highways crying
    "Who'll beyond the hills away?"

Towns and countries woo together,
    Forelands beacon, belfries call;
Never lad that trod on leather
    Lived to feast his heart with all.

Up, lad; thews that lie and cumber
    Sunlit pallets never thrive;
Morns abed and daylight slumber
    Were not meant for man alive.

Clay lies still, but blood's a rover;
    Breath's a ware that will not keep.
Up, lad: when the journey's over
    There'll be time enough to sleep.

Gerard Manley Hopkins (1844–1889)

from A Psalm of Life

Tell me not, in mournful numbers,
 "Life is but an empty dream!"
For the soul is dead that slumbers,
 And things are not what they seem.

Life is real! Life is earnest!
 And the grave is not its goal;
"Dust thou art, to dust returnest,"
 Was not spoken of the soul.

Not enjoyment, and not sorrow,
 Is our destined end or way;
But to act, that each to-morrow
 Find us farther than to-day.

Art is long, and Time is fleeting,
 And our hearts, though stout and brave,
Still, like muffled drums, are beating
 Funeral marches to the grave.

In the world's broad field of battle,
 In the bivouac of Life,
Be not like dumb, driven cattle!
 Be a hero in the strife!

Trust no Future, howe'er pleasant!
 Let the dead Past bury its dead!
Act—act in the living present!
 Heart within, and God o'erhead!

Lives of great men all remind us
    We can make our lives sublime,
And, departing, leave behind us
    Footprints on the sands of time;

Footprints, that perhaps another,
    Sailing o'er life's solemn main,
A forlorn and shipwrecked brother,
    Seeing, shall take heart again.

Let us, then, be up and doing,
    With a heart for any fate;
Still achieving, still pursuing,
    Learn to labor and to wait.

Henry Wadsworth Longfellow (1807–1882)

'I hoped that, with the brave and strong'

I hoped that, with the brave and strong
    My portioned task might lie;
To toil amid the busy throng,
    With purpose pure and high.

Anne Brontë (1820–1849)

Song CXXXIII

Fond Love, no more
    Will I adore
Thy feignèd Deity;
Go throw thy darts
    At simple hearts,
And prove thy victory.

Whiles I do keep
My harmless sheep
    Love hath no power on me:
'Tis idle souls
Which he controls;
The busy man is free.

Thomas Forde (c. 1660)

An Eastern Orthodox Morning Prayer to St Makary the Great

To thee, O Master that lovest all men, I hasten on rising from sleep; By thy mercy I go forth to do thy works, and I make my prayer to thee to help me at all times and in all things; deliver me from every evil thing of this world and from the pursuit of the devil; save me and bring me to thy eternal Kingdom. For thou art my Creator, thou dost inspire and vouchsafe every thought of good; in thee is all my hope, and to thee I ascribe glory, now and for ever, and unto the ages of ages. Amen.

Anon.

Song *from* Patient Grissill

Art thou poor, yet hast thou golden slumbers?
   Oh sweet content!
Art thou rich, yet is thy mind perplexed?
   Oh punishment!
Dost thou laugh to see how fools are vexed
To add to golden numbers, golden numbers?
Oh sweet content! Oh sweet content!
    Work apace, apace, apace, apace;
    Honest labour bears a lovely face;
   Then hey nonny nonny, hey nonny nonny!

Canst drink the waters of the crispèd spring?
   Oh sweet content!
Swim'st thou in wealth, yet sink'st in thine own tears?
   Oh punishment!
Then he that patiently want's burden bears
No burden bears, but is a king, a king!
Oh sweet content! Oh sweet content!
    Work apace, apace, apace, apace;
    Honest labour bears a lovely face;
   Then hey nonny nonny, hey nonny nonny!

Thomas Dekker (c. 1570–c. 1632)

PERSEVERANCE

Travelling

One leg in front of the other,
One leg in front of the other,
    As the little dog travelled
    From London to Dover.
And when he came to a stile–
    Jump! he went over.

Anon.

Mother to Son

Well, son, I'll tell you:
Life for me ain't been no crystal stair.
It's had tacks in it,
And splinters,
And boards torn up,
And places with no carpet on the floor–
Bare.
But all the time
I's been a-climbin' on,
And reachin' landins,
And turnin' corners,
And sometimes goin' in the dark
Where there ain't been no light.
So boy, don't you turn back.
Don't you set down on the steps
'Cause you finds it's kinder hard.
Don't you fall now–
For I's still goin', honey,
I's still climbin',
And life for me ain't been no crystal stair.

Langston Hughes (c. 1902–1967)

Don't Give Up

If you've tried and have not won,
    Never stop for crying;
All that's great and good is done
    Just by patient trying.

If by easy work you beat,
    Who the more will prize you?
Gaining victory from defeat,
    That's the test that tries you.

Phoebe Cary (1824–1871)

Upon the Snail

She goes but softly, but she goeth sure;
    She stumbles not as stronger creatures do:
Her journey's shorter, so she may endure
    Better than they which do much further go.

She makes no noise, but stilly seizeth on
    The flower or herb appointed for her food,
The which she quietly doth feed upon,
    While others range, and gare, but find no good.

And though she doth but very softly go,
    However 'tis not fast, nor slow, but sure;
And certainly they that do travel so,
    The prize they do aim at, they do procure.

John Bunyan (1628–1688)

A Noiseless Patient Spider

A noiseless patient spider,
I mark'd where on a little promontory it stood
     isolated,
Mark'd how to explore the vacant vast surrounding,
It launch'd forth filament, filament, filament, out of
     itself,
Ever unreeling them, ever tirelessly speeding them.

And you O my soul where you stand,
Surrounded, detached, in measureless oceans of
     space,
Ceaselessly musing, venturing, throwing, seeking the
     spheres to connect them,
Till the bridge you will need be form'd, till the ductile
     anchor hold,
Till the gossamer thread you fling catch somewhere,
     O my soul.

Walt Whitman (1819–1892)

Perseverance

On a bed of sickness lying,
    Wounded, hopeless, ill and faint,
Robert Bruce, great King of Scotland,
    Thus began his sad complaint:

"On the field the battle's chances
    Six times have I tried in vain;
Six times turnèd, dethroned, defeated,
    To the battle-field again.

"All my valiant men are slaughtered,
    Split and shattered sword and shield,
And I feel I soon my spirit
    To my last foe, Death, must yield.

"Take the crown away, ye foemen;
    Then, O God, my spirit take,
For my hopes are past and shattered,
    And I feel my heart will break."

As the King was thus complaining,
    Praying God to end his days,
He beheld a busy spider
    Swinging in the sun's warm rays.

In the stone-arched window hanging,
    With surprising art and strength
Carries she her thread, to fasten
    To the wall its slender length.

And he saw the spider's efforts
    Every time seemed quite in vain;
Each time that she tried to reach it,
    Each time fell she back again.

Six times he beheld her newly
    Rise with unabated zeal,
Till, encouraged by her patience,
    He began new hope to feel.

"If," thought he, "the spider's efforts
    At the seventh time succeed,
I my few remaining soldiers
    To the battle-field will lead."

Once more sideways swung the spider,
    And this time she gained the day:
Who is true and persevering,
    To despair need ne'er give way.

With new courage from his bed sprang
    Robert Bruce, the hero brave—
Once more saw his foes with terror
    Scotland's banner o'er them wave.

And with bold determination,
    Kept he still his aim in view—
Like the spider, never halted
    Till his work was finished too;

Till upon the throne in splendour
    Once again he took his place;
Then the spider he remembered
    As the saviour of his race.

And he told his sons the story—
    Told his sons and grandsons too—
How the Bruce's fame and glory
    To the spider's work is due.

Anon.

Try Try Again

'Tis a lesson you should heed,
If at first you don't succeed,
Try, try again;

Then your courage should appear,
For if you will persevere,
You will conquer, never fear
Try, try again;

Once or twice, though you should fail,
If you would at last prevail,
Try, try again;

If we strive, 'tis no disgrace
Though we do not win the race;
What should you do in the case?
Try, try again;

If you find your task is hard,
Time will bring you your reward,
Try, try again;

All that other folks can do,
Why, with patience, should not you?
Only keep this rule in view:
Try, try again.

T. H. Palmer

The Coming of Good Luck

So good luck came, and on my roof did light
Like noiseless snow, or as the dew of night:
Not all at once, but gently, as the trees
Are by the sunbeams tickled by degrees.

Robert Herrick (1591–1674)

Let No One Steal Your Dreams

Let no one steal your dreams
Let no one tear apart
The burning of ambition
That fires the drive inside your heart.

Let no one steal your dreams
Let no one tell you that you can't
Let no one hold you back
Let no one tell you that you won't.

Set your sights and keep them fixed
Set your sights on high
Let no one steal your dreams
Your only limit is the sky.

Let no one steal your dreams
Follow your heart
Follow your soul
For only when you follow them
Will you feel truly whole.

Set your sights and keep them fixed
Set your sights on high
Let no one steal your dreams
Your only limit is the sky.

Paul Cookson (1961–)

It Couldn't Be Done

Somebody said that it couldn't be done
But he with a chuckle replied
That "maybe it couldn't," but he would be one
Who wouldn't say so till he'd tried.
So he buckled right in with the trace of a grin
On his face. If he worried he hid it.
He started to sing as he tackled the thing
That couldn't be done, and he hid it.

Somebody scoffed: "Oh, you'll never do that;
At least no one ever has done it,"
But he took off his coat and he took off his hat
And the first thing we knew he'd begun it.
With a lift of his chin and a bit of a grin,
Without any doubting or quiddit,
He started to sing as he tackled the thing
That couldn't be done, and he did it.

There are thousands to tell you it cannot be done,
There are thousands to prophesy failure,
There are thousands to point out to you one by one,
The dangers that wait to assail you.
But just buckle in with a bit of a grin,
Just take off your coat and go to it;
Just start in to sing as you tackle the thing
That "cannot be done," and you'll do it.

Edgar Albert Guest (1881–1959)

I May, I Might, I Must

If you will tell me why the fen
appears impassable, I then
will tell you why I think that I
can get across it if I try.

Marianne Moore (1887–1972)

'Went to the river, couldn't get across'

Went to the river, couldn't get across,
Paid five dollars for an old gray hoss.
Hoss wouldn't pull so I traded for a bull.
Bull wouldn't holler so I traded for a dollar.
Dollar wouldn't pass so I threw it on the grass.
Grass wouldn't grow so I traded for a hoe.
Hoe wouldn't dig so I traded for a pig.
Pig wouldn't squeal so I traded for a wheel.
Wheel wouldn't run so I traded for a gun.
Gun wouldn't shoot so I traded for a boot.
Boot wouldn't fit so I thought I'd better quit.
So I quit.

Anon.

from Poor Richard's Almanac

Little strokes
Fell great oaks.

Benjamin Franklin (1706–1790)

EMPATHY

'Throughout the world'

Throughout the world if it were sought,
    Fair words enough a man shall find;
They be good cheap, they cost right nought,
    Their substance is but only wind.
But well to say and so to mean,
That sweet accord is seldom seen.

Sir Thomas Wyatt (1503–1542)

'If I can stop one heart from breaking'

If I can stop one heart from breaking,
I shall not live in vain;
If I can ease one life the aching,
Or cool one pain,
Or help one fainting robin
Unto his nest again,
I shall not live in vain.

Emily Dickinson (1830–1886)

Abou Ben Adhem

Abou Ben Adhem (may his tribe increase!)
Awoke one night from a deep dream of peace,
And saw within the moonlight in his room,
Making it rich, and like a lily in bloom,
An Angel, writing in a book of gold;
Exceeding peace had made Ben Adhem bold,
And to the presence in the room he said,
"What writest thou?"—The vision raised its head,
And with a look made of all sweet accord,
Answer'd, "The names of those who love the Lord."
"And is mine one?" said Abou. "Nay, not so,"
Replied the angel. Abou spoke more low,
But cheerily still; and said, "I pray thee, then,
Write me as one that loves his fellowmen."
The angel wrote and vanish'd. The next night
It came again, with a great wakening light,
And show'd the names whom love of God had bless'd,
And, lo! Ben Adhem's name led all the rest.

Leigh Hunt (1784–1859)

from The Song of Hiawatha

Gitche Manito, the mighty,
The creator of the nations,
Looked upon them with compassion,
With paternal love and pity;
Looked upon their wrath and wrangling
But as quarrels among children,
But as feuds and fights of children!

Over them he stretched his right hand,
To subdue their stubborn natures,
To allay their thirst and fever,
By the shadow of his right hand;
Spake to them with voice majestic,
As the sound of far off waters
Falling into deep abysses,
Warning, chiding, spake in this wise:

'O my children! my poor children!
Listen to the words of wisdom,
Listen to the words of warning,
From the lips of the Great Spirit,
From the Master of Life who made you!
I have given you lands to hunt in,
I have given you streams to fish in,
I have given you bear and bison,
I have given you roe and reindeer,
I have given you brant and beaver,
Filled the marshes full of wild-fowl,
Filled the rivers full of fishes;
Why then are you not contented?
Why then will you hunt each other?

I am weary of your quarrels,
Weary of your wars and bloodshed,
Weary of your prayers for vengeance,
Of your wranglings and dissensions;
All your strength is in your union,
All your danger is in discord;
Therefore be at peace henceforward,
And as brothers live together.'

Henry Wadsworth Longfellow (1807–1882)

from Ye Wearie Wayfarer

Question not, but live and labour
    Till yon goal be won,
Helping every feeble neighbour,
    Seeking help from none;
Life is mostly froth and bubble,
    Two things stand like stone,
Kindness in another's trouble,
    Courage in your own.

Adam Lindsay Gordon (1833–1870)

'Not, how did he die, but how did he live?'

Not, how did he die, but how did he live?
Not, what did he gain, but what did he give?
These are the units to measure the worth
Of a man as a man, regardless of birth.
Not what was his church, nor what was his creed?
But had he befriended those really in need?
Was he ever ready, with word of good cheer,
To bring back a smile, to banish a tear?
Not what did the sketch in the newspaper say,
But how many were sorry when he passed away?

Anon.

A Pilgrim's Way

I do not look for holy saints to guide me on my way,
Or male and female devilkins to lead my feet astray.
If these are added, I rejoice—if not, I shall not mind,
So long as I have leave and choice to meet my
    fellow-kind.
     For as we come and as we go (and deadly-soon
      go we!)
     The people, Lord, Thy people, are good enough
      for me!

Thus I will honour pious men whose virtue shines so
    bright
(Though none are more amazed than I when I by
    chance do right),
And I will pity foolish men for woe their sins have
    bred
(Though ninety-nine per cent. of mine I brought on
    my own head).
     And, Amorite or Eremite, or General Averagee,
     The people, Lord, Thy people, are good enough
      for me!

And when they bore me overmuch, I will not shake
    mine ears,
Recalling many thousand such whom I have bored to
    tears.
And when they labour to impress, I will not doubt nor
    scoff;
Since I myself have done no less and—sometimes
    pulled it off!

Yea, as we are and we are not, and we pretend
　　to be,
The people, Lord, Thy people, are good enough
　　for me!

And when they work me random wrong, as oftentimes
　　hath been,
I will not cherish hate too long (my hands are none
　　too clean).
And when they do me random good I will not feign
　　surprise;
No more than those whom I have cheered with
　　wayside courtesies.
　　But, as we give and as we take—whate'er our
　　　　takings be--
　　The people, Lord, Thy people, are good enough
　　　　for me!

But when I meet with frantic folk who sinfully declare
There is no pardon for their sin, the same I will not
　　spare
Till I have proved that Heaven and Hell which in our
　　hearts we have
Show nothing irredeemable on either side the grave.
　　For as we live and as we die--if utter Death there be—
　　The people, Lord, Thy people, are good enough
　　　　for me!

Deliver me from every pride—the Middle, High, and
　　Low—
That bars me from a brother's side, whatever pride he
　　show.
And purge me from all heresies of thought and speech
　　and pen

That bid me judge him otherwise than I am judged.
    Amen!
That I may sing of Crowd or King or road-borne
    company,
That I may labour in my day, vocation and degree,
To prove the same by deed and name, and hold
    unshakenly
(Where'er I go, whate'er I know, whoe'er my
    neighbour be)
This single faith in Life and Death and to Eternity:
"The people, Lord, Thy people, are good enough
    for me!"

Rudyard Kipling (1865–1936)

The Reconcilement

Come, let us now resolve at last
    To live and love in quiet;
We'll tie the knot so very fast
    That Time shall ne'er untie it.

The truest joys they seldom prove
    Who free from quarrels live;
'Tis the most tender part of love
    Each other to forgive.

When least I seem'd concern'd, I took
    No pleasure nor no rest;
And when I feign'd an angry look,
    Alas! I loved you best.

Own but the same to me—you'll find
    How blest will be our fate.
O to be happy—to be kind—
    Sure never is too late!

Sir John Sheffield,
Duke of Buckinghamshire (1648–1721)

Leonardo

Leonardo, painter, taking
    Morning air
        On Market Street
Saw the wild birds in their cages
    Silent in
        The dust, the heat.

Took his purse from out his pocket
    Never questioning
        The fee,
Bore the cages to the green shade
    Of a hill-top
        Cypress tree.

'What you lost,' said Leonardo,
    'I now give to you
        Again,
Free as noon and night and morning,
    As the sunshine,
        As the rain.'

And he took them from their prisons,
    Held them to
        The air, the sky;
Pointed them to the bright heaven.
    'Fly!' said Leonardo.
        'Fly!'

Charles Causley (1917–2003)

The Art of Being Kind

So many gods, so many creeds,
So many paths that wind and wind,
While just the art of being kind
Is all the sad world needs.

Ella Wheeler Wilcox (1850–1919)

WISDOM

Be True *from* Hamlet

This above all:
To thine own self be true,
And it must follow, as the night the day
Thou cans't not then be false to any man.

William Shakespeare (c. 1564–1616)

Love After Love

The time will come
when, with elation,
you will greet yourself arriving
at your own door, in your own mirror,
and each will smile at the other's welcome,

and say, sit here. Eat.
You will love again the stranger who was your self.
Give wine. Give bread. Give back your heart
to itself, to the stranger who has loved you

all your life, whom you ignored
for another, who knows you by heart.
Take down the love letters from the bookshelf,

the photographs, the desperate notes,
peel your own image from the mirror.
Sit. Feast on your life.

Derek Walcott (1930–2017)

I Thank You Lord

I thank you Lord, for knowing me
    better than I know myself,
And for letting me know myself
    better than others know me.
Make me, I ask you then,
    better than others know me.
Make me, I ask you then,
    better than they suppose,
And forgive me for what they do not know.

Anon.

I stepped from plank to plank

I stepped from plank to plank,
A slow and cautious way;
The stars about my head I felt,
About my feet the sea.

I knew not but the next
Would be my final inch.
This gave me that precarious gait
Some call experience.

Emily Dickinson (1830–1886)

The Tailspin

Going into a tailspin
in those days meant curtains.
No matter how hard you pulled back on the stick
the nose of the plane wouldn't come up.

Spinning round, headed for a target of earth,
the whine of death in the wing struts,
instinct made you try to pull out of it that way, by
    force,
and for years aviators spiraled down and crashed.

Who could have dreamed that the solution
to this dreaded aeronautical problem
was so simple?
Every student flier learns this nowadays:
You move the joystick in the direction of the spin
and like a miracle the plane stops turning
and you are in control again
to pull the nose up out of the dive.

In panic we want to push the stick away from the
    spin,
wrestle the plane out of it,
but the trick is, as in everything,
to go with the turning willingly,
rather than fight, give in, go with it,
and that way come out of your tailspin whole.

Edward Field (1924–)

Life

Let us be like a bird, one instant lighted
    Upon a twig that swings;
He feels it yield—but sings on, unaffrighted,
    Knowing he hath his wings!

Victor Hugo (1802–1885)

The Winds of Fate

One ship drives east and another drives west
    With the selfsame winds that blow.
        'Tis the set of the sails
        And not of the gales
    Which tells us the way to go.

Like the winds of the sea are the ways of fate,
    As we voyage along through life;
        'Tis the set of the soul
        That decides its goal,
    And not the calm or the strife.

Ella Wheeler Wilcox (1850–1919)

from Young and Old

When I was a greenhorn and young,
And wanted to be and to do,
I puzzled my brains about choosing my line,
Till I found out the way that things go.

The same piece of clay makes a tile,
A pitcher, a taw, or a brick:
Dan Horace knew life; you may cut out a saint,
Or a bench, from the self-same stick.

The urchin who squalls in a gaol,
By circumstance turns out a rogue;
While the castle-bred brat is a senator born,
Or a saint, if religion's in vogue.

We fall on our legs in this world,
Blind kittens, tossed in neck and heels:
'Tis Dame Circumstance licks Nature's cubs into
    shape,
She's the mill-head, if we are the wheels.

Then why puzzle and fret, plot and dream?
He that's wise will just follow his nose;
Contentedly fish, while he swims with the stream;
'Tis no business of his where it goes.

Charles Kingsley (1819–1875)

I have always known

I have always known
That at last I would
Take this road, but yesterday
I did not know that it would be today.

Ariwara no Narihira (825–880)

The Mountain and The Squirrel

The mountain and the squirrel
Had a quarrel,
And the former called the latter 'Little prig';
Bun replied,
'You are doubtless very big,
But all sorts of things and weather
Must be taken in together
To make up a year,
And a sphere.
And I think it no disgrace
To occupy my place.
If I'm not so large as you,
You are not so small as I,
And not half so spry:
I'll not deny you make
A very pretty squirrel track.
Talents differ; all is well and wisely put;
If I cannot carry forests on my back,
Neither can you crack a nut.'

Ralph Waldo Emerson (1803–1882)

He Who Knows

He who knows not, and knows not that he knows not,
    is a fool. Shun him;
He who knows not, and knows that he knows not,
    is a child. Teach him.
He who knows, and knows not that he knows,
    is asleep. Wake him.
He who knows, and knows that he knows, is wise.
    Follow him.

Anon.

The Pessimist

Nothing to do but work,
    Nothing to eat but food,
Nothing to wear but clothes,
    To keep one from going nude.

Nothing to breathe but air,
    Quick as a flash 'tis gone;
Nowhere to fall but off,
    Nowhere to stand but on.

Nothing to comb but hair,
    Nowhere to sleep but in bed,
Nothing to weep but tears,
    Nothing to bury but dead.

Nothing to sing but songs,
    Ah, well, alas! alack!
Nowhere to go but out,
    Nowhere to come but back.

Nothing to see but sights,
    Nothing to quench but thirst,
Nothing to have but what we've got.
    Thus through life we are cursed.

Nothing to strike but a gait;
    Everything moves that goes.
Nothing at all but common sense
    Can ever withstand these woes.

B. J. King (1857–1894)

Another Spring

If I might see another Spring
    I'd not plant summer flowers and wait:
I'd have my crocuses at once,
My leafless pink mezereons,
      My chill-veined snow-drops, choicer yet
      My white or azure violet,
Leaf-nested primrose; anything
    To blow at once, not late.

If I might see another Spring
    I'd listen to the daylight birds
That build their nests and pair and sing,
Nor wait for mateless nightingale;
      I'd listen to the lusty herds,
      The ewes with lambs as white as snow,
I'd find out music in the hail
    And all the winds that blow.

If I might see another Spring—
    Oh stinging comment on my past
That all my past results in "if"—
    If I might see another Spring
I'd laugh to-day, to-day is brief;
I would not wait for anything:
      I'd use to-day that cannot last,
      Be glad to-day and sing.

Christina Rossetti (1830–1894)

The First Step

The young poet Evmenis
complained one day to Theocritos:
'I've been writing for two years now
and I've composed only one idyll.
It's my single completed work.
I see, sadly, that the ladder
of Poetry is tall, extremely tall;
and from this first step I'm standing on now
I'll never climb any higher.'
Theocritos retorted: 'Words like that
are improper, blasphemous.
Just to be on the first step
should make you happy and proud.
To have reached this point is no small achievement:
what you've done already is a wonderful thing.
Even this first step
is a long way above the ordinary world.
To stand on this step
you must be in your own right
a member of the city of ideas.
And it's a hard, unusual thing
to be enrolled as a citizen of that city.
Its councils are full of Legislators
no charlatan can fool.
To have reached this point is no small achievement:
what you've done already is a wonderful thing.'

C. P. Cavafy (1863–1933)
translated by Edmund Keeley and Philip Sherrard

For Every Evil

For every evil under the sun
There is a remedy or there is none.
If there be one, seek till you find it;
If there be none, never mind it.

Anon.

PERSPECTIVE

Two Men Looked Out

Two men looked out through prison bars;
The one saw mud, the other stars.

Anon.

On the Beach at Night Alone

On the beach at night alone,
As the old mother sways her to and fro singing her
    husky song,
As I watch the bright stars shining, I think a thought
    of the clef of the universes and of the future,

A vast similitude interlocks all,
All spheres, grown, ungrown, small, large, suns,
    moons, planets,
All distances of place however wide,
All distances of time, all inanimate forms,
All souls, all living bodies though they be ever so
    different, or in different worlds,
All gaseous, watery, vegetable, mineral processes, the
    fishes, the brutes,
All nations, colours, barbarisms, civilisations,
    languages,
All identities that have existed or may exist on this
    globe, or any globe,
All lives and deaths, all of the past, present, future,
This vast similitude spans them, and always has
    spann'd,
And shall for ever span them and compactly hold and
    enclose them.

Walt Whitman (1819–1892)

To See a World

To see a world in a grain of sand
And a heaven in a wild flower,
Hold Infinity in the palm of your hand
And Eternity in an hour.

William Blake (1757–1827)

Of Many Worlds in This World

Just like as in a nest of boxes round,
degrees of sizes in each box are found:
So, in this world, may many others be
Thinner and less, and less still by degree:
Although they are not subject to our sense,
A world may be no bigger than two-pence.
Nature is curious, and such works may shape,
Which our dull senses easily escape:
For creatures, small as atoms, may be there,
If every one a creature's figure bear.
If atoms four, a world can make, then see
What several worlds might in an ear-ring be:
For, millions of those atoms may be in
The head of one small, little, single pin.
And if thus small, then ladies may well wear
A world of worlds, as pendents in each ear.

Margaret Cavendish (1623–1673)

It is not growing like a tree

It is not growing like a tree
In bulk, doth make Man better be;
Or standing long an oak, three hundred year,
To fall a log at last, dry, bald, and sere:
      A lily of a day
      Is fairer far in May,
   Although it fall and die that night;
   It was the plant and flower of Light.
In small proportions we just beauties see;
And in short measures life may perfect be.

Ben Jonson (1572–1637)

The Brook

I come from haunts of coot and hern,
    I make a sudden sally,
And sparkle out among the fern,
    To bicker down a valley.

By thirty hills I hurry down,
    Or slip between the ridges,
By twenty thorps, a little town,
    And half a hundred bridges.

Till last by Philip's farm I flow
    To join the brimming river,
For men may come and men may go,
    But I go on for ever.

I chatter over stony ways,
    In little sharps and trebles,
I bubble into eddying bays,
    I babble on the pebbles.

With many a curve my banks I fret
    By many a field and fallow,
And many a fairy foreland set
    With willow-weed and mallow.

I chatter, chatter, as I flow
    To join the brimming river,
For men may come and men may go,
    But I go on for ever.

I wind about, and in and out,
    With here a blossom sailing,
And here and there a lusty trout,
    And here and there a grayling.

And here and there a foamy flake
    Upon me, as I travel
With many a silvery waterbreak
    Above the golden gravel,

And draw them all along, and flow
    To join the brimming river,
For men may come and men may go,
    But I go on for ever.

I steal by lawns and grassy plots,
    I slide by hazel covers;
I move the sweet forget-me-nots
    That grow for happy lovers.

I slip, I slide, I gloom, I glance,
    Among my skimming swallows;
I make the netted sunbeam dance
    Against my sandy shallows.

I murmur under moon and stars
    In brambly wildernesses;
I linger by my shingly bars;
    I loiter round my cresses;

And out again I curve and flow
    To join the brimming river,
For men may come and men may go,
    But I go on for ever.

Alfred, Lord Tennyson (1809–1892)

Beginning

It is to be found half-way between sleep and waking–
A starting point, a recognition, beginning.
Think of the clouds on this planet lifted away
And the stars snapped off and the day tremendously
     breaking
And everything clear and absolute, the good morning
Striking the note of the day.

So it was and so it is always and still
Whether you notice or not. Forget that you are
Eyes, nose, ears but attend. So much must go on
Daily and hourly. Wait for the morning to fill
With cockcrow and petals unfolding, the round
     planet's power
Held in the hands of the sun.

And somewhere around are presences, always have
     been
Whose hands remove clouds, whose fingers prise open
     the sun.
Watch, learn the craft of beginning and seeing the
     world
Disclose itself. Take this down to a small thing, a keen
Whisper of wind, the sound of the cock or your own
Story that waits to be told.

I stood at a window once. I was four or five
And I watched the sun open the garden and spread
     out the grass
And heard the far choir of some blackbirds and
     watched blue flowers rise.

This was the first day for me, the planet alive
And I watched the stars' shadows grow faint and
    finally pass
And I could not believe my eyes.

Elizabeth Jennings (1926–2001)

from Childe Harold's Pilgrimage

There is a pleasure in the pathless woods,
    There is a rapture on the lonely shore,
There is society where none intrudes,
    By the deep sea, and music in its roar.
    I love not man the less, but Nature more,
From these our interviews, in which I steal
    From all I may be, or have been before,
To mingle with the universe, and feel
What I can ne'er express, yet can not all conceal.

George Gordon, Lord Byron (1788–1824)

Fearless Bushmen

The bushmen of the Kalahari desert
Painted themselves on rocks
With wildebeests and giraffes
Thousands of years ago.
And still today they say
To boast is sinful
Arrogance is evil.
And although some say today that they
Are the earliest hunter-gatherers known
They never hunt for sport
They think that's rude,
They hunt for food.
They earn respect by sharing
Being true to their word
And caring.
They refuse to own land but
They can build a house in two days
And take it down in four hours.

Three generations will live together.
A girl will grow up to feed her mother
Who feeds the mother
That once fed her.
To get that food a girl will walk
Upon the hot desert sands
An average of a thousand miles a year.
Their footprints are uniquely small
For people who travel so much
To find melons or mongongo trees,
And those small dark and nimble feet
May spend two days chasing a deer.

Charity, respect and tolerance
Are watchwords for these ancient folk
Who spend their evenings singing songs
Around their campfires.

These hunter-gatherers are fearless
But peaceful,
They will never argue with a mamba snake,
When one is seen heading towards the village
They kiss the Earth
And move the village.

Benjamin Zephaniah (1958–)

A Day of Sunshine

O gift of God! O perfect day:
Whereon shall no man work, but play;
Whereon it is enough for me,
Not to be doing, but to be!

Through every fibre of my brain,
Through every nerve, through every vein,
I feel the electric thrill, the touch
Of life, that seems almost too much.

I hear the wind among the trees
Playing celestial symphonies;
I see the branches downward bent,
Like keys of some great instrument.

And over me unrolls on high
The splendid scenery of the sky,
Where through a sapphire sea the sun
Sails like a golden galleon,

Towards yonder cloud-land in the West,
Towards yonder Islands of the Blest,
Whose steep sierra far uplifts
Its craggy summits white with drifts.

Blow, winds! and waft through all the rooms
The snow-flakes of the cherry-blooms!
Blow, winds! and bend within my reach
The fiery blossoms of the peach!

O Life and Love! O happy throng
Of thoughts, whose only speech is song!
O heart of man! canst thou not be
Blithe as the air is, and as free?

Henry Wadsworth Longfellow (1807–1882)

The Tangled Skein

Try we life-long, we can never
    Straighten out life's tangled skein,
Why should we, in vain endeavour,
    Guess and guess and guess again?
      Life's a pudding full of plums;
      Care's a canker that benumbs.
Wherefore waste our elocution
On impossible solution?
Life's a pleasant institution,
    Let us take it as it comes!

Set aside the dull enigma,
    We shall guess it all too soon;
Failure brings no kind of stigma—
    Dance we to another tune!
      String the lyre and fill the cup,
      Lest on sorrow we should sup;
Hop and skip to Fancy's fiddle,
Hands across and down the middle—
Life's perhaps the only riddle
    That we shrink from giving up!

W. S. Gilbert (1836–1911)

The Rainy Day

The day is cold, and dark, and dreary;
It rains, and the wind is never weary;
The vine still clings to the mouldering wall,
But at every gust the dead leaves fall,
    And the day is dark and dreary.

My life is cold, and dark, and dreary;
It rains, and the wind is never weary;
My thoughts still cling to the mouldering Past,
But the hopes of youth fall thick in the blast,
    And the days are dark and dreary.

Be still, sad heart! and cease repining;
Behind the clouds is the sun still shining;
Thy fate is the common fate of all,
Into each life some rain must fall,
    Some days must be dark and dreary.

Henry Wadsworth Longfellow (1807–1882)

The Optimist and the Pessimist

Twixt the optimist and pessimist
The difference is droll;
The optimist sees the doughnut,
The pessimist sees the hole.

McLandburgh Wilson (c. 1892)

CONTENTMENT

Pippa's Song

The year's at the spring,
And day's at the morn;
Morning's at seven;
The hill-side's dew-pearled;
The lark's on the wing;
The snail's on the thorn:
God's in his heaven—
All's right with the world!

Robert Browning (1812–1889)

The Ted Williams Villanelle

(for Ari Badaines)

'Don't let anybody mess with your swing.'
                                    Ted Williams, baseball player

Watch the ball and do your thing.
This is the moment. Here's your chance.
Don't let anybody mess with your swing.

It's time to shine. You're in the ring.
Step forward, adopt a winning stance,
Watch the ball and do your thing,

And while that ball is taking wing,
Run, without a backward glance.
Don't let anybody mess with your swing.

Don't let envious bastards bring
You down. Ignore the sneers, the can'ts.
Watch the ball and do your thing.

Sing out, if you want to sing.
Jump up, when you long to dance.
Don't let anybody mess with your swing.

Enjoy your talents. Have your fling.
The seasons change. The years advance.
Watch the ball and do your thing,
And don't let anybody mess with your swing.

Wendy Cope (1945–)

Self-Pity

I never saw a wild thing
sorry for itself.
A small bird will drop frozen dead from a bough
without ever having felt sorry for itself.

D. H. Lawrence (1885–1930)

The Pobble

The Pobble who has no toes
    Had once as many as we;
When they said, "Some day you may lose them all,"
    He replied, "Fish fiddle-de-dee!"
And his Aunt Jobiska made him drink
Lavender water tinged with pink,
For she said, "The World in general knows
There's nothing so good for a Pobble's toes!"

The Pobble who has no toes
    Swam across the Bristol Channel;
But before he set out he wrapped his nose
    In a piece of scarlet flannel,
For his Aunt Jobiska said, "No harm
Can come to his toes if his nose is warm;
And it's perfectly known that a Pobble's toes
Are safe – provided he minds his nose!"

The Pobble swam fast and well,
    And when boats or ships came near him,
He tinkledy-binkledy-winkled a bell,
    So that all the world could hear him,
And all the Sailors and Admirals cried,
When they saw him nearing the further side,
"He has gone to fish for his Aunt Jobiska's
Runcible Cat with crimson whiskers!"

But before he touched the shore,
    The shore of the Bristol Channel,
A sea-green Porpoise carried away
    His wrapper of scarlet flannel,

And when he came to observe his feet,
Formerly garnished with toes so neat,
His face at once became forlorn
On perceiving that all his toes were gone.

And nobody ever knows,
        From that dark day to the present,
Whoso had taken the Pobble's toes,
        In a manner so far from pleasant.
Whether the shrimps or crawfish grey,
Or crafty mermaids stole them away –
Nobody knew; and nobody knows
How the Pobble was robbed of his twice five toes.

The Pobble who has no toes
        Was placed in a friendly Bark,
And they rowed him back, and they carried him up
        To his Aunt Jobiska's Park.
And she made him a feast at his earnest wish
Of eggs and buttercups fried with fish: –
And she said, "It's a fact the whole world knows
That Pobbles are happier without their toes."

Edward Lear (1812–1888)

Song *from* The Winter's Tale

Jog on, jog on, the footpath way,
    And merrily hent the stile-a;
A merry heart goes all the day,
    Your sad tires in a mile-a.

William Shakespeare (c. 1564–1616)

Solitude

Laugh, and the world laughs with you,
Weep, and you weep alone;
For the sad old earth must borrow its mirth,
But has trouble enough of its own.
Sing, and the hills will answer,
Sigh, it is lost on the air;
The echoes bound to a joyful sound,
But shrink from voicing care.

Rejoice, and men will seek you,
Grieve, and they turn and go;
They want full measure of all your pleasure,
But they do not need your woe.
Be glad, and your friends are many,
Be sad, and you lose them all;
There are none to decline your nectared wine,
But alone you must drink life's gall.

Feast, and your halls are crowded,
Fast, and the world goes by.
Succeed and give, and it helps you live,
But no man can help you die;
For there is room in the halls of pleasure
For a long and lordly train,
But one by one we must all file on
Through the narrow aisles of pain.

Ella Wheeler Wilcox (1850–1919)

To my Sister

It is the first mild day of March:
Each minute sweeter than before,
The redbreast sings from the tall larch
That stands beside our door.

There is a blessing in the air,
Which seems a sense of joy to yield
To the bare trees, and mountains bare,
And grass in the green field.

My sister! ('tis a wish of mine)
Now that our morning meal is done,
Make haste, your morning task resign;
Come forth and feel the sun.

Edward will come with you – and pray,
Put on with speed your woodland dress;
And bring no book: for this one day
We'll give to idleness.

William Wordsworth (1770–1850)

Eternity

He who binds to himself a joy
Does the winged life destroy;
But he who kisses the joy as it flies
Lives in eternity's sun rise.

William Blake (1757–1827)

from Song of the Open Road

Afoot and light-hearted I take to the open road,
Healthy, free, the world before me,
The long brown path before me leading me wherever
    I choose.

Henceforth I ask not good-fortune, I myself am
    good-fortune.
Henceforth I whimper no more, postpone no more,
    need nothing,
Done with indoor complaints, libraries, querulous
    criticisms,
Strong and content I travel the open road.

Walt Whitman (1819–1892)

Contentment

Get hence, foul Grief, the canker of the mind;
Farewell, Complaint, the miser's only pleasure;
Away, vain Cares, by which few men do find
      Their sought-for treasure.

Ye helpless sighs, blow out your breath to nought;
Tears, drown yourselves, for woe your cause is wasted;
Thought, think to end—too long the fruit of thought
      My mind hath tasted.

But thou, sure Hope, tickle my leaping heart,
Comfort, step thou in place of wonted sadness;
Fore-felt Desire, begin to savour part
      Of coming gladness.

Let voice of sighs into clear music run;
Eyes, let your tears with gazing now be mended;
Instead of thought true pleasure be begun,
      And never ended.

Philip Sidney (1554–1586)

Wood Rides

Who hath not felt the influence that so calms
The weary mind in summers sultry hours
When wandering thickest woods beneath the arms
Of ancient oaks and brushing nameless flowers
That verge the little ride who hath not made
A minutes waste of time and sat him down
Upon a pleasant swell to gaze awhile
On crowding ferns bluebells and hazel leaves
And showers of lady smocks so called by toil
When boys sprote gathering sit on stulps and weave
Garlands while barkmen pill the fallen tree
—Then mid the green variety to start
Who hath [not] met that mood from turmoil free
And felt a placid joy refreshed at heart

John Clare (1793–1864)

from To a Skylark

Hail to thee, blithe spirit!
    Bird thou never wert,
That from heaven, or near it,
    Pourest thy full heart
In profuse strains of unpremeditated art.

Higher still and higher
    From the earth thou springest
Like a cloud of fire;
    The blue deep thou wingest,
And singing still dost soar, and soaring ever singest.

In the golden lightning
    Of the setting sun,
O'er which clouds are brightening,
    Thou dost float and run
Like an unbodied joy whose race is just begun.
        [...]
Teach us, sprite or bird,
    What sweet thoughts are thine:
I have never heard
    Praise of love or wine
That panted forth a flood of rapture so divine.
        [...]
What objects are the fountains
    Of thy happy strain?
What fields, or waves, or mountains?
    What shapes of sky or plain?
What love of thine own kind? what ignorance of pain?

With thy clear keen joyance
    Langour cannot be:
Shadow of annoyance
    Never came near thee:
Thou lovest; but ne'er knew love's sad satiety.

Waking or asleep,
    Thou of death must deem
Things more true and deep
    Than we mortals dream,
Or how could thy notes flow in such a crystal stream?

We look before and after,
    And pine for what is not:
Our sincerest laughter
    With some pain is fraught;
Our sweetest songs are those that tell of saddest
    thought.

Yet if we could scorn
    Hate, and pride, and fear;
If we were things born
    Not to shed a tear,
I know not how thy joy we ever should come near.

Better than all measures
    Of delightful sound,
Better than all treasures
    That in books are found,
Thy skill to poet were, thou scorner of the ground!

Teach me half the gladness
        That thy brain must know,
Such harmonious madness
        From my lips would flow,
The world should listen then, as I am listening now.

Percy Bysshe Shelley (1792–1822)

Happy the Man

Happy the man and happy he alone,
    He who can call today his own:
    He who, secure within, can say,
Tomorrow do thy worst, for I have lived today.
    Be fair or foul or rain or shine
The joys I have possessed, in spite of fate, are mine.
Not Heaven itself upon the past has power,
But what has been, has been, and I have had my
    hour.

John Dryden (1631–1700)

GOOD ADVICE

Every Day

Love the beautiful,
    Seek out the true,
Wish for the good,
    And the best do!

Moses Mendelssohn (1729–1786)

Desiderata

Go placidly amid the noise and the haste,
and remember what peace there may be in silence.
As far as possible, without surrender,
be on good terms with all persons.
Speak your truth quietly and clearly;
and listen to others, even to the dull and the ignorant;
they too have their story.
Avoid loud and aggressive persons;
they are vexatious to the spirit.

If you compare yourself with others,
you may become vain or bitter,
for always there will be greater and lesser persons
     than yourself.
Enjoy your achievements as well as your plans.
Keep interested in your own career, however humble;
it is a real possession in the changing fortunes of time.

Exercise caution in your business affairs,
for the world is full of trickery.
But let this not blind you to what virtue there is;
many persons strive for high ideals,
and everywhere life is full of heroism.

Be yourself. Especially do not feign affection.
Neither be cynical about love;
for in the face of all aridity and disenchantment,
it is as perennial as the grass.

Take kindly the counsel of the years,
gracefully surrendering the things of youth.

Nurture strength of spirit to shield you in sudden
    misfortune.
But do not distress yourself with dark imaginings.
Many fears are born of fatigue and loneliness.

Beyond a wholesome discipline, be gentle with
    yourself.
You are a child of the universe no less than the trees
    and the stars;
you have a right to be here.
And whether or not it is clear to you,
no doubt the universe is unfolding as it should.

Therefore be at peace with God,
whatever you conceive Him to be.
And whatever your labors and aspirations,
in the noisy confusion of life, keep peace in your soul.
With all its sham, drudgery and broken dreams,
it is still a beautiful world.
Be cheerful. Strive to be happy.

Max Ehrmann (1872–1945)

Consider Beginnings *from* Tao Te Ching

Do without doing.
Act without action.
Savor the flavorless.
Treat the small as large,
the few as many.

Meet injury
with the power of goodness.

Study the hard while it's easy.
Do big things while they're small.
The hardest jobs in the world start out easy,
the great affairs of the world start small.

So the wise soul,
by never dealing with great things,
gets great things done.

Now, since taking things too lightly makes them
    worthless,
and taking things too easy makes them hard,
the wise soul,
by treating the easy as hard,
doesn't find anything hard.

Lao Tzu (c. 500 BCE)
translated by Ursula Le Guin

Ecclesiastes 3:1–8 *from* the King James Bible

To every thing there is a season,
    and a time to every purpose under heaven:
A time to be born, and a time to die;
    a time to plant, and a time to pluck up that
        which is planted;
A time to kill, and a time to heal;
    a time to break down, and a time to build up;
A time to weep, and a time to laugh;
    a time to mourn, and a time to dance;
A time to cast away stones, and a time to gather
    stones together;
    a time to embrace, and a time to refrain from
        embracing;
A time to get, and a time to lose;
    a time to keep, and a time to cast away;
A time to rend, and a time to sew;
    a time to keep silence, and a time to speak;
A time to love, and a time to hate;
    a time of war, and a time of peace.

Anon.

If—

If you can keep your head when all about you
    Are losing theirs and blaming it on you;
If you can trust yourself when all men doubt you,
    But make allowance for their doubting too;
If you can wait and not be tired by waiting,
    Or, being lied about, don't deal in lies,
Or, being hated, don't give way to hating,
    And yet don't look too good, nor talk too wise;

If you can dream—and not make dreams your master;
    If you can think—and not make thoughts your
        aim;
If you can meet with triumph and disaster
    And treat those two impostors just the same;
If you can bear to hear the truth you've spoken
    Twisted by knaves to make a trap for fools,
Or watch the things you gave your life to broken,
    And stoop and build 'em up with wornout tools;

If you can make one heap of all your winnings
    And risk it on one turn of pitch-and-toss,
And lose, and start again at your beginnings
    And never breathe a word about your loss;
If you can force your heart and nerve and sinew
    To serve your turn long after they are gone,
And so hold on when there is nothing in you
    Except the Will which says to them: "Hold on";

If you can talk with crowds and keep your virtue,
    Or walk with kings—nor lose the common touch;
If neither foes nor loving friends can hurt you;

If all men count with you, but none too much;
If you can fill the unforgiving minute
    With sixty seconds' worth of distance run—
Yours is the Earth and everything that's in it,
    And—which is more—you'll be a Man, my son!

Rudyard Kipling (1865–1936)

Lord of Himself

How happy is he born or taught
    Who serveth not another's will;
Whose armour is his honest thought,
    And simple truth his highest skill;

Whose passions not his masters are;
    Whose soul is still prepared for death –
Not tied unto the world with care
    Of prince's ear or vulgar breath;

Who hath his ear from rumours freed;
    Whose conscience is his strong retreat;
Whose state can neither flatterers feed,
    Nor ruin make oppressors great;

Who envies none whom chance doth raise,
    Or vice; who never understood
How deepest wounds are given with praise,
    Nor rules of state but rules of good;

Who God doth late and early pray
    More of his grace than gifts to lend,
And entertains the harmless day
    With a well-chosen book or friend –

This man is free from servile bands
    Of hope to rise or fear to fall:
Lord of himself, though not of lands,
    And, having nothing, yet hath all.

Sir Henry Wotton (1568–1639)

Sayings of the Buddha

This is the noble truth of the way that leads to the cessation of pain: it is the Noble Eightfold Path, namely: Right views, Right intention, Right speech, Right action, Right livelihood, Right effort, Right mindfulness, Right concentration.

This Noble Eightfold Path is to be practised.

The Things That Count

Count your garden by the flowers,
never by the leaves that fall.
Count your days by garden hours,
don't remember clouds at all.
Count your nights by stars, not shadows.
Count your years with smiles, not tears.
Count your blessings, not your troubles.
Count your age by friends, not by years.

Anon.

Some of the hurts you have cured

Some of the hurts you have cured,
And the sharpest you still have survived,
But what torments of grief you endured
From evils which never arrived!

Ralph Waldo Emerson (1803–1882)

from The Church Porch

By all means use sometimes to be alone.
Salute thy self: see what thy soul doth wear.
Dare to look in thy chest, for 'tis thine own:
And tumble up and down what thou find'st there.
    Who cannot rest till hee good-fellows finde,
    He breaks up house, turns out of doores his minde.

Be thriftie, but not covetous: therefore give
Thy need, thine honour, and thy friend his due.
Never was scraper brave man. Get to live;
Then live, and use it: els, it is not true
    That thou hast gotten. Surely use alone
    Makes money not a contemptible stone.
        [...]
Catch not at quarrels. He that dares not speak
Plainly and home, is coward of the two.
Think not thy fame at ev'ry twitch will break:
By great deeds shew, that thou canst little do;
    And do them not: that shall thy wisdome be;
    And change thy temperance into braverie.
        [...]
Wit's an unruly engine, wildly striking
Sometimes a friend, sometimes the engineer.
Hast thou the knack? pamper it not with liking:
But if thou want it, buy it not too deere.
    Many, affecting wit beyond their power,
    Have got to be a deare fool for an houre.
        [...]
Envie not greatnesse: for thou mak'st thereby
Thy self the worse, and so the distance greater.
Be not thine own worm: yet such jealousie,

As hurts not others, but may make thee better,
    Is a good spurre. Correct thy passions spite;
    Then may the beasts draw thee to happy light.
                    [...]
Be usefull where thou livest, that they may
Both want and wish thy pleasing presence still,
Kindnesse, good parts, great places are the way
To compasse this. Finde out mens wants and will,
    And meet them there. All worldly joyes go lesse
    To the one joy of doing kindnesses.
                    [...]
Pitch thy behaviour low, thy projects high;
So shalt thou humble and magnanimous be:
Sink not in spirit: who aimeth at the sky,
Shoots higher much then he that means a tree.
    A grain of glorie mixt with humblenesse
    Cures both a fever and lethargicknesse.
                    [...]
Summe up at night, what thou hast done by day;
And in the morning, what thou hast to do.
Dresse and undresse thy soul: mark the decay
And growth of it: if with thy watch, that too
    Be down, then winde up both; since we shall be
    Most surely judg'd, make thy accounts agree.

In brief, acquit thee bravely; play the man.
Look not on pleasures as they come, but go.
Deferre not the least vertue: lifes poore span
Make not an ell, by trifling in thy wo.
    If thou do ill; the joy fades, not the pains:
    If well; the pain doth fade, the joy remains.

George Herbert (1593–1633)

from Tao Te Ching

In dwelling, live close to the ground.
In thinking, keep to the simple.
In conflict, be fair and generous.
In governing, don't try to control.
In work, do what you enjoy.
In family life, be completely present.

Lao Tzu (c. 500 BCE)
translated by Stephen Mitchell

from Lines to Mr Hodgson

Now at length we're off for Turkey,
    Lord knows when we shall come back!
Breezes foul and tempests murky
    May unship us in a crack.
But, since life at most a jest is,
    As philosophers allow,
Still to laugh by far the best is,
    Then laugh on—as I do now.
        Laugh at all things,
        Great and small things,
    Sick or well, at sea or shore;
        While we're quaffing,
        Let's have laughing—
Who the devil cares for more?—
Some good wine! and who would lack it,
Ev'n on board the Lisbon Packet?

George Gordon, Lord Byron (1788–1824)

Index of Poets

Index of Titles

Index of First Lines

Permissions Acknowledgements

Permissions Acknowledgements

with The Permissions Company, LLC on behalf of Shambhala Publications, Inc., www.shambhala.com.

'In dwelling, live close to the ground' from *Tao Te Ching: A New English Version* by Stephen Mitchell. Translation copyright © 1988 by Stephen Mitchell. Used by permission of HarperCollins Publishers.

MACMILLAN COLLECTOR'S LIBRARY

Own the world's great works of literature in one beautiful collectible library

Designed and curated to appeal to book lovers everywhere, Macmillan Collector's Library editions are small enough to travel with you and striking enough to take pride of place on your bookshelf. These much-loved literary classics also make the perfect gift.

Beautifully produced with gilt edges, a ribbon marker, bespoke illustrated cover and real cloth binding, every Macmillan Collector's Library hardback adheres to the same high production values.

Discover something new or cherish your favourite stories with this elegant collection.

Macmillan Collector's Library: own, collect, and treasure

Discover the full range at
macmillancollectorslibrary.com